I Am Rosie:
I Hear You

First Edition published 2025 by

2QT Limited (Publishing)

United Kingdom

Copyright © Frank English 2025

The right of Frank English to be identified as the author of this work has been asserted by him in accordance with the Copyright, Designs and Patents Act 1988

All rights reserved. This book is sold subject to the condition that no part of this book is to be reproduced, in any shape or form. Or by way of trade, stored in a retrieval system or transmitted in any form or by any means, electronic, mechanical, photocopying, recording, be lent, re-sold, hired out or otherwise circulated in any form of binding or cover other than that in which it is published and without a similar condition, including this condition being imposed on the subsequent purchaser, without prior permission of the copyright holder.

Printed in Great Britain by IngramSpark

A CIP catalogue record for this book is available from the British Library

ISBN 978-1-9193271-4-3

I Am Rosie:
I Hear You

by Frank English

with Rosie, Becky and Stuart Brown

Time Changes Everything

Every day is special — but the birth of your child is something truly extraordinary.

Rosie had been named before she was even born, having arrived on Valentine's Day 2012, a week early, by planned Caesarean section. A calm and peaceful baby even in the womb — no somersaults or kicks like her active sister, Isabel — Rosie seemed relaxed and content from the very start.

Then came the moment she was gently brought into the world. Rosie took it all in her stride — she didn't even cry. She simply looked around with her inquisitive eyes, quietly taking everything in. From the moment I saw her, I couldn't stop saying, "She's perfect. Isn't she perfect?" Little did we know what was waiting around the corner.

Rosie didn't pass her newborn hearing test, but the nurse reassured us that this was normal — probably just some remaining amniotic fluid. Then, at three months old, after many follow-up tests, we learned that Rosie was profoundly deaf. It came as a huge shock.

But Rosie's life — and who she is — has never been defined by her deafness, nor by being on the autistic spectrum. Time truly changes everything. With Rosie's determination, and our unwavering support, time has shaped her journey — from managing her deafness to adapting to the effects of her cochlear implants, which were completely unknown to us at the beginning.

Rosie underwent a six-hour surgery to receive her implants — the gift that allowed her to hear. She then spent several years in speech and language therapy, and we are now seeking support for her recent ARFID eating diagnosis.

Some days are hard, especially at school — struggling to hear in noisy environments, feeling frustrated when people get tired of repeating themselves and say "What's wrong? Are you deaf?"

Or finding it impossible to learn when she's overwhelmed, exhausted, or suffering headaches from anxiety.

However, through it all, Rosie has never given up. Her resilience shines through — most recently when she became a World Champion in Tae Kwon-do in her category.

We tell Rosie every day how proud we are of her — not just for her achievements, but simply for getting through each day with courage and grace. She is loving, caring, beautiful, determined, and guided by a strong moral compass.

To us, Rosie has always been — and always will be — absolutely perfect.

Chapter 1

"She's perfect, Stuart. Isn't she perfect in every detail?" Becky suggested to her husband as she cuddled her new-born daughter very gently, stroking her head of luscious lightly coloured brown hair as she gazed into those quizzical blue eyes, as gentle tears rolled almost carefully down her cheeks.

"Have you noticed that she's … not … crying?" Stuart pointed out cautiously. "She seems to be trying really hard to focus on what she can see within this room. Is that what—?"

"Babies do?" Becky added, a gently questioning look crossing *her* face. "She hadn't cried much at all even when she first arrived. I just gave birth to my most beautiful baby daughter, as most mothers do."

The room fell inordinately still with all eyes fixed on this rather quiet and unusually inquisitive tiny face whose unblinking eyes imbued her with a strangely ethereal look that no-one seemed to understand. Didn't *all* newly born babies *cry* endlessly once exposed to air and somewhat strange creatures that did nothing but smile and make odd shapes with their face?

"She's been booked in for all the tests that hospitals put new babies through," Becky informed him, "and—"

"Tests?" her mother asked, unsure what she was hearing. "How do you mean … tests? Surely you can't be saying there might be something … wrong?"

"She's a baby!" Becky's mother stated sharply. "How is she going to pass any tests? She's not been long born, for goodness' sake!"

"It's what they do," Becky insisted calmly – how could she be so steady when questioned about something she knew nothing about when all she wanted to do was love her adorable infant? "They know what they are doing … and I'm not about to gainsay the way they handle new-borns. *Don't* you think she's beautiful?"

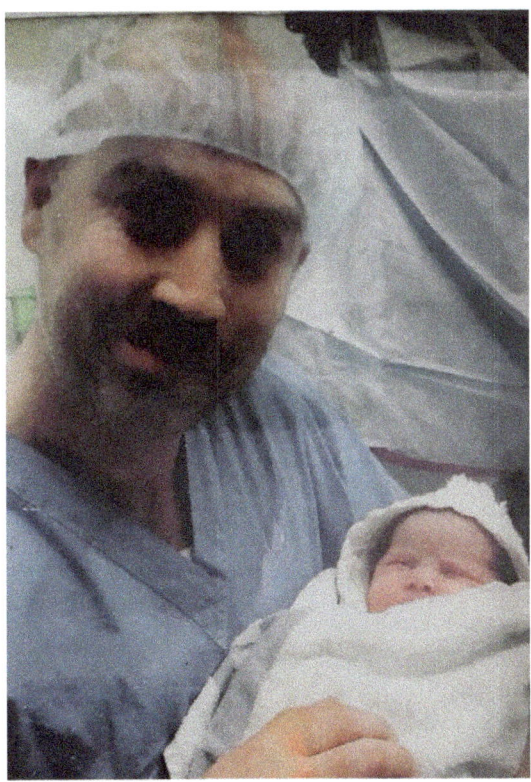

Here she is! Just arrived.

-o-

"We always perform what we call 'new-born hearing screening'," the nurse began to explain. "This allows us to probe further to check if there might be any deficiencies in the child's ability to … hear."

"Are you trying to tell me that my new-born child might possibly be … deaf?" Becky gasped, panic rising in her throat.

"It's probably only some residue of amniotic fluid in her channels," the nurse assured. "With no history of deafness in your family … There is no such history, I assume?"

"I don't think so!" Becky reacted, alarmed at the suggestion. "I'm not sure, but I don't think there is deafness anywhere in the family."

"Then, we will book Rosie in for further tests in around three months' time," the nurse rejoined after an embarrassing silence had descended, exacerbated by the doubts now swirling around Becky's confused mind. "She seems to be all right in most other areas."

"Most?" Becky queried, her mind jumping into a different direction. "Does that mean that there might be … 'other' things wrong with our dear daughter?"

"Mrs Brown," the newly arrived Yorkshire doctor addressed Becky's confused and almost alarmed questioning. "All new-born nippers are assessed as time goes along because we are not able to read their mind. They are all confused bundles of humanity that can be assessed for more functions the more sophisticated they become. Ostensibly – and I use that word advisedly – we begin to recognise more about their developmental issues as they grow. I wouldn't worry. She seems to be a beautifully normal human being."

Becky smiled nervously, a glistening tear beginning to show in her confused eye. She drew her unprotesting bundle of joy close to her bosom as she kissed her unblinking eyes gently. What was going on behind those large blue windows into her mind Becky had no idea. All she was bothered about was that her dear little bundle was here and … breathing.

Chapter 2

"Do you think our little treasure's … deaf, Stuart?" Becky asked her husband, quite at a loss as to what to think in the weeks after the nurse and doctor's original opinions at their local hospital. "I mean … she's only just arrived, and babies don't learn to do more than cry until they're a lot older. Do they?"

"Don't forget that nothing much more than a whimper or a gurgle comes from her mouth," he responded almost disheartened by the prospect. "Do you notice, however, how she takes in everything that happens around her?"

"How do you mean?" Becky replied with a puzzled frown.

"Eyes wide and unblinking whenever she is somewhere … different?" he went on. "'Soaking' up new stuff … silently? No noise at all. Almost as if she's *processing* mentally – making her *own* decisions about stuff."

'What is going on behind those deep, blue windows into that young mind?' Becky thought as she lifted Rosie from her crib. Could her little daughter be *so* deep? Not a sound escaped her lips as she settled in her mother's arms close to her breast. However, those unblinking eyes followed her every move, waiting to see what was going to happen next.

"Well," Becky shrugged, "this afternoon's exhaustive testing should give us at least *some* answers, although I am sure I don't know what sorts of tests they are about to do other than banging drums and clapping loudly."

"Is it really twelve weeks that we've had her?" Stuart gasped, unable to comprehend that their Big Test Day had arrived so quickly, almost taking them by surprise. "What on earth are the medics going to surprise us with? That she's from another planet?"

Baby Rosie with no hearing (Age 2/3 months)

"Good morning!" a pleasant Scottish female voice greeted Becky as she settled into the hospital's waiting room with her daughter. "My, what a beautiful young lady you have there! Ready for our batch of tests?"

"Not sure," Becky replied, still confused as to why they were there. It had been a fraught and puzzling few weeks for her and her husband, as they tried to explain how they wanted to solve their daughter's perceived problems by devising their own – inadequate – tests. The suggestion that Rosie might have a hearing problem brought a certain degree of denial to Becky's mind.

"Clapping loudly or making noises will never work with someone that has hearing problems, if that's what we are about to assess," the audiologist explained. "You will probably realise that Rosie's reactions to your walking into her room are down to her observation skills of being able to see you rather than hear you. Anyway, we will know the truth by the end of today."

-o-

"What do you mean when you say she hasn't passed the ninety-decibel test?" Becky asked the audiologist after several hours of seemingly pointless tests.

"Ninety decibels would be the noise produced by a Jumbo Jet or a pneumatic drill," the audiologist explained. "In other words, she is—"

"Profoundly ... deaf?" Becky added, tears beginning to collect. "Can she not have ... hearing aids fitted?"

"She could quite easily," the audiologist butted in. "It would allow us to see if there is any residual hearing. The strong likelihood is that she may fiddle with them, but that's a risk we could take."

"So ... why might she be deaf?" Becky asked, at a loss for an answer.

"Why might she be deaf when you and your husband are not?" came the reply. "We will do further tests – on you and your husband as well – because there is a possibility her condition may depend on genetics."

"And what does that mean?" Becky asked, needing answers she could understand.

"It means the condition might have been caused by her inheritance of the condition from ... you, your husband, or ... both of you," the stark response dropped in her lap.

"So does that mean she could be deaf ... forever?" Becky gasped, tears beginning to gather.

"Indeed," the audiologist explained, "but there are things we might be able to do to alleviate the problem. It all depends on certain physical conditions."

"Which are?" Becky queried, concerned there might be much more she wouldn't understand.

"Whether this new response we might be able to make would be physically ... possible," came the answer slowly.

"If so?" Rebecca asked again, hopefully positively.

"Good news ... possibly," the audiologist responded with a smile.

"And if not?" Rebecca went on, cautiously slowly.

"Not such good news," was the reply. "However, let's not get ahead of ourselves. We'll examine all our options once we have them before us."

-o-

Becky sat quietly on her own in the waiting area once the audiologist had gone, raw emotions playing with her mind. Her one overriding question returned to her again and again – why had her beautiful baby been visited with *these* problems that no-one else in her knowledge had to experience?

Was there something during her pregnancy that she had done to cause this to happen? Had she overlooked some important advice that had been offered that would have taken away all this worry?

There hadn't been any physical problems when she had brought her other daughter, Isabel, into the world. Explaining such problems to *her* hopefully wouldn't prove to be too difficult. She felt sure they would all get along even though normal communication might be an issue.

'What could the responses be that the audiologist covertly suggested?' Becky wondered to herself, puzzled that they might have to accept that Rosie would never be … normal.

The door clicked open, jerking her from the depths of her despair.

"I didn't mean to startle you," a deep male voice offered apologetically. "I am Rosie's consultant."

Chapter 3

"Mummy?" seven-year-old Isabel asked quietly as they sat over a cup of tea in the kitchen. "What does 'cochlea' mean and how does it apply to our Rosie? Is it something she will have to do to learn to talk? I know she's only a few months old, but she doesn't even make any sounds much, except for blowing the occasional … raspberry."

"I'm seven and even I can't do that!" Isabel added with a disappointed grimace after a moment or two's quiet.

"Her difficulties are nothing she is doing wrong," Becky replied slowly as she sat between Isabel and her other daughter, Lauren, on the settee in their comfy sitting room. "We have been told that she is … deaf."

Silence followed as she cast non-understanding and frowned glances at her mother.

"Do you understand what this means?" her mother asked carefully slowly, seeing that her daughter's reaction reinforced her ignorance. "It means that she was born not able to hear any sounds at all."

"But…" Isabel replied carefully, "she blows … raspberries," Isabel added quickly. "How can she do that if she can't hear?"

"I believe it's to do with the vibration it causes in her mouth," Mum tried to explain, only just able to understand it herself.

Almost immediately the seven-year-old tried to prove it, making a funny if different sound with her tongue.

"No, not like that," Becky urged in her attempt to make her understand because of her puzzlement. "Put your fingers in your ears … and then try it."

A look of utter surprise and shock leaped into her face at the result.

"And she can't hear—?" Isabel gasped finding it hard to grasp the concept just brought to her mind by her mother. "Only … feel?"

"How will we be able to talk to her when she is old enough?" she went on after a few moments of careful thought. "Will we be able … to say 'hello', even?" she added not really comprehending the difficulties, as she had started talking a little before she had reached her second birthday anniversary.

"That's what the doctors are about to do," Becky started to explain. "There's something deep in her ear linked to Rosie's brain – all our brains – called a cochlea. When it detects sounds in a normal person, it vibrates and sends its messages to the brain. There is no such link in Rosie's head, hence her not being able to hear."

Isabel had fallen silent, trying to take in and understand all her mum was saying.

"So," she began to ask slowly, "why hasn't *she* got one, but we have."

"For some reason," Becky tried to explain carefully, "it seems like she might have inherited the problem from one of our – her – ancestors."

"An … sess … ters?" Isabel sounded the word slowly that she didn't understand.

"People like grandparents or great-grandparents, I suppose," Becky replied quite simply. "I'll be able to tell you more when I have spoken to the doctors concerned."

-o-

"This is all so difficult to understand," Becky's mum, Deborah, puzzled. "Can I assume that there is no history of this sort of thing in any of the family?"

"You would perhaps know that better than anyone else, Mum," Becky responded. "The consultant has referred Rosie to the cochlear implant clinic."

"And what is that when it's at home?" Deborah asked with a sceptically puzzled look.

"Well…" Becky began the explanation that Rosie's consultant had given to her, who had referred her to see if Rosie might be able to have implants allowing her to hear.

"They have asked, too, if you and Dad might be available at some time," she went on to a look of surprise and shock etched on her mum's face. "They would like you to give a blood sample at some stage so they might be able to trace the origin of Rosie's problem. Would that be all right with you?"

Silent nods indicated Rosie's grandparents' agreement, much to Becky's relief.

"I'll let you all know when they inform me of time and place," Becky added, a relieved look covering her face.

"How will they know whether Rosie has this … cochlea thingy?" Frank asked with a shrug.

"She'll have an MRI scan when we get there to make sure," Becky assured him.

"And if she doesn't … have this cochlea thing?" her dad asked pointedly.

"Then none of this will happen and Rosie will remain totally deaf, without hearing anything for the rest of her life," Becky muttered quietly as tears threatened.

"Fingers crossed then," Frank added with a false but placatory grin. He knew what all this meant to his daughter, because *she* believed, for some reason, that *blame* lay at *her* doorstep for all Rosie was about to endure.

Chapter 4

"Are you sure you're all right?" Stuart asked his wife while they waited for their hoped-for visit to the cochlear implant centre. Although she had been very active showing Rosie love and activities that didn't rely on sound or language, Rosie had had ordinary hearing aids fitted. As expected, she loved to tug them out and to play with them.

"A bit concerned really," Becky replied as she sat down with her cup of tea in the living room of the flat they usually rented for a stay they loved in Pembrokeshire.

"About?" he asked, not sure where this line was heading.

"If Rosie can do *that* with her hearing aids," she added as her baby daughter had examined an aid she had unhitched and thrown out of her cot, "then what will she do with her cochleae? £7,000 is a lot of cash for us to fork out for any she might destroy."

"She's not going to do that," Stuart interjected, trying to assure her, although the amount to replace just one of the instruments had startled him more than a little.

"Then how are they going to make sure they stay where they are put?" Becky ventured, genuinely unsure. "Sit all day and watch her?"

"I think she is sensible enough to do as we ask," Stuart offered. "After all, she is going on for her first birthday. We'll have to see."

Unexpectedly, the telephone interrupted their conversation.

Becky gathered it tentatively from its cradle in the hallway, not sure who wanted to catch her at their stay in Wales.

"Are you going to tell me what that was all about?" Stuart asked eager to know. "Someone eager to contact us?"

"Early next week," she uttered as she picked up her waiting cup of luke-warm tea.

"Next week what?" he asked, surprised at her lack of detail.

"The cochlear implant centre – second visit," she continued "They have a cancellation giving us less time to wait. Five weeks before Rosie's birthday."

-o-

"OK," Becky muttered to her husband as they waited quietly in the implant centre's waiting area. Unblinking and without sound, Rosie sat on her lap keenly watching their moving mouth as they held their cautious conversation. "I know it's a way off, but deciding on schooling will be a worrying issue at some time in the next couple of years."

"Why do we need to think about *that now*?" Stuart responded. "She's not yet one, for goodness' sake!"

"Most youngsters that I know of start nursery schooling at about three," Becky urged. "Do you know of any schools where we live that can take children who can't hear?"

His mouth closed tightly, unable to rationalise clearly. He hadn't thought about that and so thought it only sensible not to pursue it.

"Hello. Good morning," an educated voice greeted them as the waiting area door clicked shut behind it. "I am your hearing consultant, and this must be … Rosie? What a lovely smile."

Raspberry girl.

Immediately, Rosie replied with a rasping raspberry that brought a smile to Becky's face, but a huge smile and spontaneous guffaw from the consultant. He could see the slightly resigned look in Becky's eyes and surprise across her husband's face straight away.

"No need for embarrassment, Mrs Brown," the medic interjected with a dismissive wave of the hand. "This is very often how we communicate upon our first meeting! It is good to see she can understand what the 'raspberry' is all about."

His returned raspberry to Rosie surprised her parents, but not her as she grinned widely and let out a truncated chuckle, recognising the vibration she felt close by.

"Several things we need to do today," he went on, sitting close to Rosie as he listened to her chest through his stethoscope. "We need to discuss her condition, explaining all the whys and wherefores, along with arranging for a handful of 'hearing' tests to be absolutely certain there is no hint of any natural hearing within her systems."

"But why?" Becky asked, eager to know why some natural hearing might not be a useful bonus. "Wouldn't that make things easier to rectify?"

"Establishing a link with Rosie's cochleae without interference from even the slightest 'natural' residue is vitally important," the consultant explained. "Anyway, any slight residue would be wiped out throughout the process."

Looking into their eyes quietly for a moment or two convinced him they understood and were ready to continue.

"If I can ask you to follow me," he began as he headed for the door, "we'll get started on Rosie's journey to our hearing world."

Chapter 5

"It's difficult to forecast where Rosie's deafness has come from," the consultant observed. "We believe there are four options, covering around fifty percent, with another fifty percent unknown. It may well be because of a genetic inheritance."

"How will we know?" Becky asked with a puzzled look decorating her face.

"We will need to do tests on your blood to ascertain those reasons," he responded.

"Blood tests?" she queried.

"Yes," he answered. "On all three of you – mum, dad and … Rosie. I think also it will be necessary for her to undergo an MRI scan to make sure she has a couple of cochleae allowing her to have the implants fitted."

"And if there are no cochleae in place?" Becky asked, nervous about the answer.

"Implants would be impossible," the consultant stated baldly.

Eager to get the processes under way but nervous non-the-less, Becky and Stuart had to wait patiently for the results once the scan had been completed, from ignorance to cochlear implant.

Fortunately, that result wasn't long in coming. She most definitely had both cochleae which allowed her to have grommets fitted to make sure her ears were clear before the big operation.

About three months after Rosie had been diagnosed as deaf, the Browns were introduced to a very helpful lady who turned out to be a teacher of the deaf, which they never knew existed in the real world. She became their guide through all the difficult passages, accompanying them to future implant appointments, connecting them with other families in similar situations, and helping them to navigate this brave new world.

A number of weeks after the blood tests the family received the shock results that Rosie's deafness was genetic. This had come about because Rosie's parents had been identified as carriers of Connexin 26 and 30 which were mutated genes that didn't allow certain proteins to be made that make cells to carry sound to the brain. Cochlear implants replaced those cells with electrodes that allowed that process to be achieved.

The decision to allow the implant process to go ahead was a big one, but once everything was in place, Becky and Stuart couldn't wait for the operation to come around. This would welcome their lovely Rosie into their hearing world.

Chapter 6

"Big day today," Becky said to her daughter as she lifted her for a hug and a kiss. "Two weeks to go to the first anniversary of the day you were born but today is another celebration that you won't understand until it's done."

The hospital seemed busy but strangely quiet as if everyone knew both what was about to happen with Rosie and how important the operation would be for her. Having been told how long the operation might be, once she had been trundled down to the theatre after sedation, the unreal waiting time began.

Apart from the occasional entry and exit of the odd person or two, the waiting room seemed unreal and in another world. Stuart and Becky talked very little during the ultimate six hour wait, each no doubt consumed with their own feelings and worries. The outcome of the operation was, at this stage, unsure. It could only be given an even chance of success. As usual, only time would tell, but throughout their period spent in the room with no indication as to how things were progressing, worries were allowed to grow.

Six hours and umpteen cups of tea or coffee later, a nurse stole into the waiting room quietly so as not to disturb anyone that might have slipped into slumber.

"The operation has been finished successfully we believe," she explained, "with Rosie coming round gradually from the anaesthetic. We will come to take you to her in a short while when she is open to seeing you."

Stuart and Becky hugged each other knowing that they would soon be able to do the same with their beloved daughter. They didn't know, of course, how successful the operation had been. Another worry until they would be able to witness for themselves.

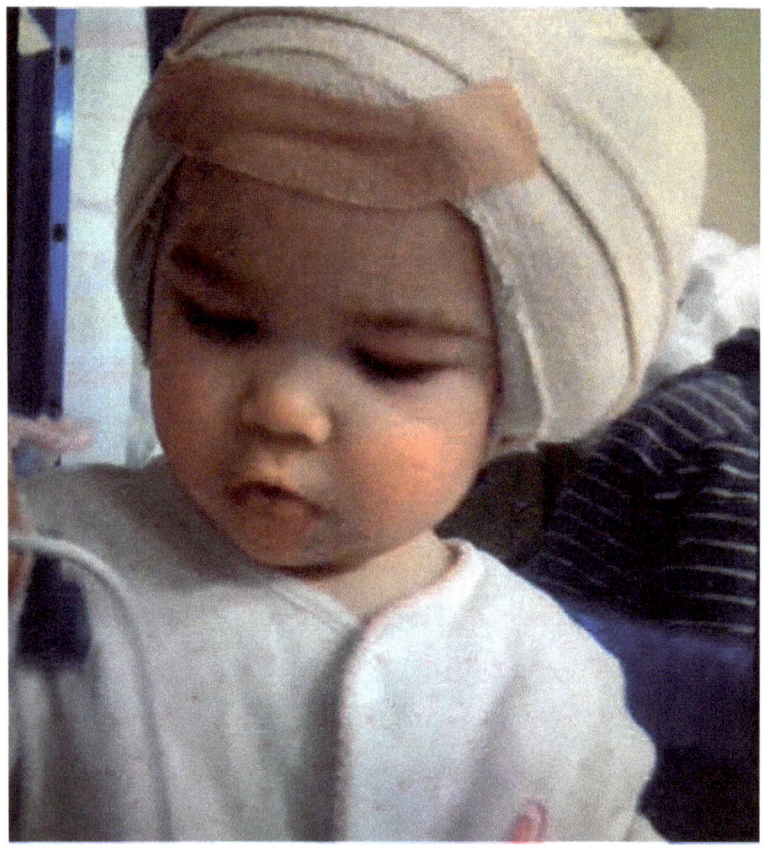

Ready with another raspberry?

What a shock when they entered the post op room to find her unusually pale-faced with her head swathed in what seemed to be an enormous bandage!

"The bandage needs to stay on for a few days to ensure the cochleae remain intact," the medic informed them. "Scars from the operation need to settle for around four weeks or so which will be checked on a number of appointments we will have to arrange. It is vitally important that you and Rosie take great care to make sure the implants remain safe.

"We will get in touch at some stage during the following weeks or so when we consider she will be ready for the switch-on."

"Switch-on?" Becky asked, a little puzzled at their meaning.

"We have to be sure the implants are secure enough for them to have an impulse passed through them to allow for the initial activation," they explained. "This activation will be very low key to avoid overwhelming Rosie. We have to bear in mind that she has been able to hear no sound at all so far in her very short life. Too much sound will not be helpful as we obviously can't warn her about what is to happen. Our world can be extremely noisy; something she has never experienced in the short time she has been with us.

"Consequently," he went on, "on successive visits, we will turn up the volume slightly, so she is not overwhelmed with what she hears."

-o-

The first anniversary of Rosie's birth arrived with great anticipation even though there would be at least another two weeks before any sound would percolate.

At this time, however, the most important celebration was her birthday party. One year on this earth! How wonderful was that! Surrounded by all the love, emotion and anticipation such a milestone can afford to the person concerned, Rosie enjoyed what her parents and close family had to offer. It was always at the back of their mind that very soon would come the most testing time of all – the implant switch-on which would decide whether she would join the vast majority of the hearing population in a different world altogether from the one to which she had grown accustomed.

Rosie's first birthday with her sister Isabel in the background

Chapter 7

The wounds from the original operation took around four weeks to heal which seemed like a lifetime. The major visit to the centre had to be for turning on and tuning in the cochleae, which was a worrying time for all the family. Would the implants work? How effective would they be? Would they cause Rosie discomfort or difficulties? All questions that provided no obvious answers.

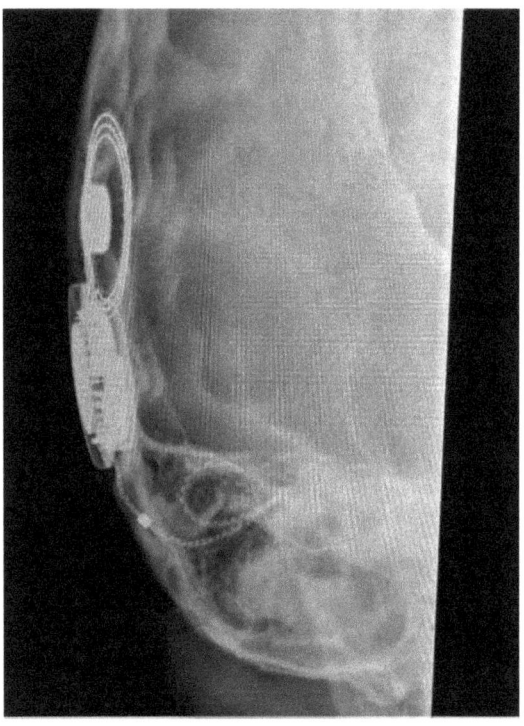

X ray of Rosie's cochlear implant

The original appointment was designed to activate the machinery to allow Rosie to start getting used to having a small amount of different activity in her brain – activity that allowed her to join in with her outside world. The initial activation was quite low to avoid her being overwhelmed by strange noises pounding in her head.

On the drive home from the initial appointment, Becky turned up the car's music system as she was eager for Rosie to experience what this sound business was all about. When she looked back at her to see how she was coping, she found that she was fast asleep, peacefully embracing the new world into which she had been lulled.

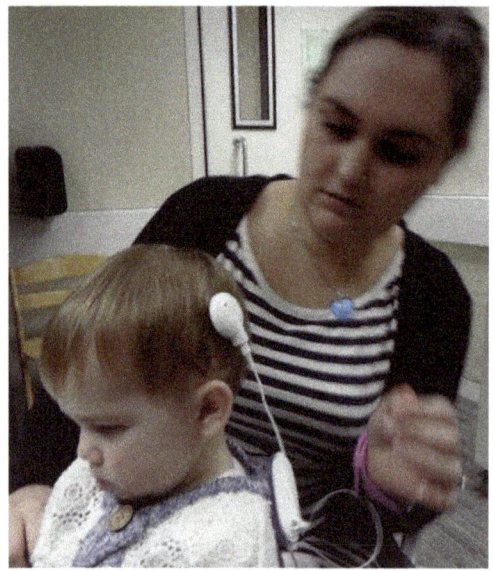

Rosie at switch-on

Following this initial implant activation, the life of the whole family was inundated with medical appointments at the implant centre during which time the volume on the devices was gradually increased, making sure Rosie wasn't startled by so many new and different sounds. For example, during hearing tests when she responded to a particular sound, on the machinery she was linked to a small monkey in a box would light up on a screen and play a drum, bringing huge smiles of joy to her face.

Although there were times when the implants 'fell off', they would bleep constantly to warn of the danger. Losing one or other of them also could result in a cost of around £7,000 per implant, causing an occasional stressful moment around the possible cost issue. Overall, however, over the following months, Rosie responded very well to wearing her implants, but was never encouraged to make any noise responses to what she experienced on a regular basis in her 'different' world. This encouraged her parents to assume she may *never* talk, which was a concerning disappointment to them. Unfortunately, there never had been any guarantee that the implants would provide a panacea for her lack of speech.

However, despite the many challenges, Rosie adapted reasonably well to her implants. It was only when she had had one or two tuning issues that she began to see the beauty of speech. One day in the tiny spare bedroom where she played and where mum and dad tried to encourage her to turn what she heard into spoken sound, that their first break through popped out of thin air.

Another check-up (Age 2)

"Bubbles," Becky said to Rosie as she blew little spheres from the plastic holder she had given her. "Bubbles, Rosie. Bubbles."

Without hesitation, staring at the bubbles and pointing as they rose towards the ceiling, Rosie replied calmly and purposefully, "Bubbles. Bubbles."

"Say again, Rosie!" Becky gasped almost unable to believe what she had heard her daughter say.

"BUBBLES!" Rosie repeated much more loudly as if she wanted the whole town to hear what she could say. "BUBBLES!"

Becky flung her arms around her and drew her giggling body to her bosom in ecstasy at hearing her daughter's first word. Would this be the start of a cascade of words from now on? Was her problem a thing of the past? Would she be able to speak properly from now on?

Or was it a one off, again leaving Mum and Dad with no further progress? They had no idea. Only further work and time would tell. Even if it had been a one off, the joy of that moment was indescribable. Even if she never spoke another word, it all seemed worth the effort, and that word gave the family hope that she was understanding their speech and that one day she might talk more.

Chapter 8

Over the next few months Rosie's vocabulary increased significantly which prompted Becky and Stuart to consider enrolling her in a local school where, hopefully, she would receive much more professional help to improve her linguistic skills.

The school chosen was a small village organisation with a one class intake. At this time Rosie was two years old.

Even though the school was small with hopefully enough time to afford Rosie extra support because of her significant needs, the powers that be therein didn't feel the local authority would support their application for the construction of an Education, Health and Care Plan (EHCP). This would have provided funding for additional one-to-one support for Rosie to make sure she was achieving positively what was necessary for improvement.

The school obviously hadn't felt it was necessary to support her lack of progress for a child of her age, even though they felt a greater degree of individual tutoring would have been beneficial bearing in mind that she recognised only five letters of the alphabet.

An independent assessment confirmed the parental concerns about her lack of progress linguistically despite educationalists being aware that this was the case. Rosie's parents considered it perhaps would be necessary to seek a better educational environment to cater for Rosie's needs as a matter of some urgency, given that her extra diagnosis of being on the autistic spectrum came at age three.

This was an additional concern for them as they had been aware up to then that she had dietary sensitivities which meant she wouldn't eat most important items like vegetables and fruits. To this end, it was felt that a move to another, more productive school might give her the support she desperately needed; a school with fewer children, less noise and a more personalised approach and attention to her needs.

Unfortunately, a few schools approached felt that Rosie was too far behind for them to provide the wherewithal for her to improve her learning skills. These rejections brought sadness and frustration to the whole family, showing them that the state system of education had failed abysmally to provide a reasoned and reasonable system of education for Rosie to improve gradually, underlining also their unwillingness to help a child of her age.

Fortunately, a small school out of the two independent schools contacted stood out as a welcoming organisation that was willing to take her in to offer her an education that others had rejected. Rosie started her journey with this school the very next day, allowing her to be herself, even with wearing her old school uniform for the time being. They also suggested that it would be smoother for her to join Reception – one year below – so she might catch up with everything she had missed.

As this school was independent of the local education authority, school fees had to be met, but they weren't excessively expensive and were affordable for Becky and Stuart.

During their conversation with the headteacher, the major question concerned the absence of an Education, Health and Care Plane was raised. He offered guidance and hope, reassuring them that Rosie needed such a plan that the school would support.

As parents of a child with special educational needs, Becky and Stuart now understood that they would have to fight for what was right for Rosie. The encouragement that they had received in this respect from this new school lifted the darkness that had been dropped upon them by other schools local to where they lived, thereby encouraging them to press the local authorities to do what was right by their daughter.

Chapter 9

Before Rosie changed schools, on 23rd July 2016, her first cousin, Monty, was born. Seemingly a perfect little boy, he was born to Becky's sister and brother-in-law, Lucy and William. Significantly, however, Monty also failed his newborn hearing tests, which indicated to Becky where *his* journey, too, might be heading. The navigation of his way through this strange silent world would prove to be very much less difficult because of what had been learned through Rosie.

Rosie with Monty in Abu Dhabi

Because of the family link between Rosie and Monty, tests were done to ascertain whether any possible physical link might have been the cause of their underlying problems. It was discovered that both families were carriers of the Connexin genes which made it a very rare occurrence.

Rosie's new school was very small with fewer than a hundred children in the age range three to eleven, giving around fifteen in her class. Although she settled in quickly and was very happy in her new environment, as time passed it became obvious that she needed more support to achieve her true potential. Over time, as well as employing a solicitor who was experienced in special educational needs to help to challenge the local education authority, further assessments were sought to build Rosie's case for a smaller learning environment.

To challenge the local authority to provide more detailed one-to-one support along with on-going assistance from a teacher of the deaf and speech and language therapy, significant financial investment as well as legal fees and school costs were necessary. The journey for Becky and Stuart turned into a steep learning curve as they were unaware of their legal rights as they fumbled in the dark for answers.

Rosie had to undergo a series of assessments including an evaluation from an educational psychologist, a teacher of the deaf, speech and language assessments and an IQ test. The results of all these tests supported their assertion for Rosie's needs so much so that by May 2019 they were completely ready for the special educational needs tribunal.

Five days before the hearing, the local educational authority conceded.

Because they had to agree that Rosie had a legal entitlement to support, the authority agreed to provide one-to-one support, to cover her speech and language therapy, and to ensure she had access to a teacher of the deaf. When in place, the stark contrast between this outcome and the struggle Rosie had had to endure in a severely noisy classroom of thirty children, without any support whatsoever was mind-blowing.

Finally, Rosie began to thrive in her new environment with her EHCP in place, enjoying her one-to-one support in the classroom and her weekly visits from a speech therapist. The future was looking ... rosy.

However, in January 2020 very concerning news began to cause thoughts of future problems as the threat of a devastating pandemic began to surface. By March that year, every child was ushered into legal isolation as the pandemic began to cause devastation throughout the known world. Rosie's course had to be put on hold, as was the case with almost all other children no matter what *their* difficulties were.

Although the severity of what was happening in the rest of the world was enormous, Becky and Stuart adapted their situation to allow for Rosie's situation to stabilise. They taught Rosie themselves, guided by her school's remote learning schedule.

Remembering this time of isolation with fondness, however, Rosie responded well to their teaching, with a spring and summer filled with playing, cooking, crafting, and, more importantly, spending precious time together.

Chapter 10

The next few years became very fragmented because, like everyone else, Rosie was in and out of school constantly. This, of course, had been caused initially by the advent of the very destructive pandemic that had arrived on the scene unexpectedly in 2020.

Rosie and her sister, Isabel (Ages 10/16)

Fortunately, Rosie handled home teaching better than her family had expected. Becky had begun to sense when she was ready to engage in learning and when she needed a break. In the necessary pauses in the education process, Becky and Rosie enjoyed together 'fun' activities like making tie-dye shirts and helping Rosie to learn how to ride her bike. It had been a case of finding a balance within which she could survive.

During these times, family was very important for Rosie where strong relationships with her family members were vitally important.

Rosie with Mum and Dad

Rosie's last two years at primary school had unfortunately become emotionally challenging for her. With a remarkably high emotional intelligence she was able to sense when something wasn't quite right, despite her special educational needs. This allowed her to rationalise and discuss situations that other youngsters may not have recognised.

Her parents decided ultimately that perhaps a move back up to her age-appropriate year group needed to be considered. This was nothing to do with her academic standing, but more about her emotional well-being. Spending her time with peers of her own age would undoubtedly enhance her mental health.

Also, the one-to-one support she had received throughout her time in this particular school had begun to taper in preparation for her move to secondary education, allowing her to experience a greater degree of independence. Unfortunately, however, Rosie took this move personally. Although she had formed a strong bond over time with her helper, Rosie's autism seemed to make her feel that her supporter didn't like her anymore.

As the time approached for her to move to senior school, the thoughts of a large school with 2,000+ pupils, including crowded classes of 30 or more students, began to cause a degree of serious dread to develop in both Rosie and her parents. Such an overwhelming fear of what would be 'normal' for a youngster with no problems began to prey on her mind.

Through research and Rosie's EHCP, a much smaller school,

thrust itself onto her horizon. Traditional, like her primary school, with about fifteen students in each year group, Rosie was drawn to it immediately following the initial visit. She even chatted with the cooks about food options which was vital owing to her limited diet and anxiety around food. She tried the flapjacks and had given them a huge 'thumbs up'. The 'Harry Potter-themed' English department was another huge plus for Rosie.

However, Becky didn't want to rely solely on this option. Important questions plagued her mind incessantly. What if the local education authority didn't agree? What if the school was full? Having Rosie's hopes dashed would be devastating for her. Were there any other schools of similar standing offering appropriate opportunities?

By fortuitous chance another school appeared on their horizon, suggested by one of Becky's acquaintances. This was an independent high school in Edgbaston.

She decided to call the school to explore the possibility of applying independently – without reference to Rosie's EHCP – as an eleven-year-old girl in her own right on her own merits. Although late for consideration, the school said they had read Rosie's special needs plan and might just be able to squeeze her in for an assessment.

Two other, similar, independent schools appeared, but the experience they offered wasn't at all positive. Because Rosie wasn't highly academic, they weren't interested in her as a person and were not able to see Rosie as she truly was. They were unable to see beyond her difficulties and to accept her for the beautiful soul she had become. As expected, Becky received cold rejection letters from these two schools, which didn't provide any surprises, probably realistically because they didn't consider her to be an intellectually gifted child because of her special educational needs.

It was a heart-breaking process trying to find a school where Rosie might be able to thrive. It felt like no-one wanted her and she might be destined to be rejected yet again. In despair, Becky took the case back to her present primary school, even asking if it might be possible for her to stay there another year. The headteacher assured her that Rosie was emotionally ready to move on.

One cold December morning, a letter arrived from the independent school in Edgbaston. Becky hesitated to open it because she didn't want Rosie to be disappointed with a possible negative response concerning her application to join the school. She had told her daughter that the other schools had been full and as a result there would be no place for her in either school.

Last chance saloon? Where to next if…?

Slowly … mind-numbingly slowly, Becky opened the letter to find that … she had done it! Rosie had been offered a place at the school for the next academic year! It was the only school out of the three independents that had not only looked at her academic successes but had also focused on her as a person.

Rosie had attended an interview where she talked about her cochlear implant because she had been born totally deaf, along with all the difficult obstacles she had had to endure and overcome. The school had even set up a mini lesson as part of the application process to see how students engaged in lessons. They were interested in the girls as individuals, not only in their test scores.

They had finally found the perfect school and Rosie had secured her place not through the local education authority, but by being herself – Rosie Brown, the incredible eleven-year-old that she is.

Chapter 11

Initially a little hesitant about attending an all-girls school, Rosie really enjoyed trying on her new school uniform, although her mum, Becky, had been rather too eager to buy it prematurely!

The arrival of her first day in this educational edifice presented a wholly new set of experiences that could have proved to be taxing. She started the senior school not knowing anyone in an environment that presented experiences she had not encountered before – the educational environment, the teachers, other children along with friendships that hopefully might come to fruition. Although these could have been overwhelming significantly for anyone, Rosie faced the possible trials head-on.

A new school with unsought-for strange experiences? Possible difficulties because of her place on the autistic spectrum? Being the only person in the organisation with cochlear implants? How would she cope?

Within her first week, the school organised an overnight stay in the school grounds that they called *Glamp 7*, where the girls camped in teepees and took part in activities designed to help them bond. A wonderful idea in essence, perhaps, but how would she cope with her severely limited diet and sleeping in absolute silence once she had removed her implants? Such sleepovers quite often might mean ghost stories and late-night gossip, but Rosie would be surrounded by total silence.

Despite all these possible 'difficulties' the school staff were wonderfully reassuring and supportive of her courage, and over time she began to settle to normal life in her new school. She even started to enjoy maths thanks to her incredible teachers!

Because Rosie had been a little unsure about being in an all-girls school, her parents decided to enrol her in a local Karate class. Her dad, Stuart, had previously earned his junior black belt years before, decided to revisit his journey in Karate with his daughter, learning with and supporting Rosie as they experienced the martial art together.

Although the family's legal journey uncovered difficulties and stumbling blocks they had to uncover and solve, Rosie finally began to thrive. This was encouraged to grow because she had at last her EHCP in place which allowed her to enjoy one-to-one support in the classroom and her weekly visits from a speech therapist. Life was beginning to improve significantly.

From January 2020, however, life threw a huge spanner in the works because of the approach of a world-wide and potentially deadly virus to humankind.

By March 2020 all school children had to take their lessons at home in isolation, afraid even to leave their homes. Fortunately, by this time Rosie had begun to find the right path for her, but unfortunately, she wasn't able to develop it publicly.

Happily, the upset didn't last long. Although the severity of what was happening publicly, with many people dying from the pandemic, was far greater than anything else imaginable, Rosie adapted to her parents' home teaching guided by the school's remote learning schedule.

The situation could have been very much more difficult, but the family remembers those times with more than a little fondness. Rosie responded well to her parents' teaching throughout the pandemic, and the spring and summer of that year were filled with playing, cooking, crafting and, most importantly, with spending precious time together.

Saundersfoot beach (Age 13)

Top left: Rosie enjoying life; Top right: Rosie in the restaurant on a cruise ship; Bottom left: New Year's Day swim in Saundersfoot dressed as an alien; Bottom right: with her golden retriever buddy.

Chapter 12

From her dad, Stuart.

Rosie has always been drawn to physical activity and the thrill of sports like martial arts and football. She thrives on movement, regularly exercising on her own – doing sit-ups, push-ups, chin-ups, and sprinting through the park. Physical activity became her personal outlet for stress, giving her a way to feel strong, capable and confident.

Her father, who also used sports as a coping tool in his youth, recognised the value it would bring to Rosie, especially as she approached her teenage years which could be emotionally turbulent.

However, she was once advised by her cochlear implant consultant to avoid contact sports due to the risk of physical trauma that could damage her implants. This felt like a heavy limitation for her on something she enjoyed doing and would be beneficial for her.

Everything changed after Rosie and her father had read an article about a professional female rugby player who wore cochlear implants and also featured on the TV programme Gladiators. Inspired, her parents raised the topic at Rosie's annual check-up, with a different consultant. He reassured them that participation in physical sports would be safe for Rosie.

This was the new guidance that opened a very important door and changed Rosie's life.

Rosie and her dad 'into' martial arts.

Mum and Dad began to look for martial arts classes that fitted in with her school schedule to make sure she wouldn't become over tired. Initially, she joined a local Karate class that allowed her to enjoy the training. Rosie also started playing football at a local park, giving her not only a chance to be active but also to socialise with boys. This was something she lacked at her all-girls school.

Although she enjoyed karate itself, Rosie found the environment challenging because of her autism and eventually decided to leave the class. Nonetheless, her enthusiasm for the sport didn't fade. So as not to lose contact with a sport she had loved, her father enrolled both himself and his daughter in a new, traditional karate class. This allowed them to train side-by-side and to share the journey, strengthening their bond and allowing them to encourage one another throughout.

This new class proved to be a turning point. The environment they found themselves in proved to be supportive but not overly aggressive, allowing them both to develop confidence and enjoy social interaction. She felt valued and began to grow her skills, which was something she hadn't experienced in her previous academic life.

At school, Rosie had often felt inferior as she struggled with deafness, autism and having average gradings. Despite recent academic progress she lacked self-confidence significantly. She was even told by peers that she wasn't as clever as them. Because deaf students often faced academic challenges, for Rosie the pressure was exacerbated by her additional needs.

Showing her a different kind of success, karate became her outlet, her motivator and her personal achievement that became something she could be proud of. Entering her first competition she competed brilliantly, facing off in a dramatic final match against a higher-grade boy opponent. In front of a cheering crowd, she earned several medals as she won her category, giving her a significant feeling of success and pride in what she had achieved.

Hoping for recognition when she returned to school the following day, the response from her peers was very disappointing. Their indifference to her personal successes was another reminder that she didn't quite fit or belong. Determined to prove to herself that she was worthy of recognition, she joined another – new – Tae Kwon-Do club where the environment was significantly unfamiliar, missing the comfort of being at a slightly higher grade in a known social circle.

The corrections she received as a beginner in this new style knocked her confidence, obliging her to stop attending for a time.

However, seduced by an approaching grading and the Midland Championships just ahead, she re-entered the 'arena'. Regular training sessions and mixing with higher grades including black belts and larger male opponents allowed her inner drive to become refuelled to improve.

She performed with remarkable composure at the Midland Championships where she reached the finals. Narrowly losing a close match re-emphasised her belief that her previous success at karate was no fluke. Surely her peers at school would now recognise her skills and successes in the field of martial arts! Unfortunately, similar indifference towards her skills prevailed throughout.

Deciding to relegate her lack of peer recognition, she continued to train diligently, and over the next year, martial arts became her lifestyle.

Crowned English Champion and earning second place in the

team competition even though this was in a higher weight and grade category, her perseverance had paid off.

English champion at Tae Kwon-Do in her height category (Age 13)

At her next grading in a large mixed group, Rosie was stunned to be named 'Best in Grading'; something that was almost unbelievable for her.

Her own philosophy?

"I can't live without sport. Tae Kwon-Do, running, football and working out all help my mental health … and they keep me fit every day."

This philosophy then led her to become the world champion in 2025 in her category.

World Champion 2025 (Age 13/14)!

World Champion!

Ultimate beach-lover!

Chapter 13

Dear Frank, this is Rosie. I would like to tell you my side of the story as I got older for you to put in the book.

Being a kid born with a mental and physical disability is not the easiest thing ever.

I was diagnosed with Autism when I was three, which was not a big surprise though because my sister had it as well. I was born profoundly deaf and due to that alone I missed out on a lot of learning. It's quite a big surprise how much you could pick up in your first year of life.

My parents enrolled me in a public school but due to background noise in the classroom I could never really learn properly. I was there until halfway through Year One because my parents had come to the realisation that I needed a learning environment with fewer children because fewer kids mean less noise. So, they searched and found a small independent school which was 20 minutes away from our house.

My mum and I went to have a look at it. Realising I was mentally and physically challenged, the headteacher suggested to my mum that I perhaps needed to have an educational, health and care plan from the local authority. My parents thought that was a brilliant idea, so they fought for one and won. So, from a young age I have been an EHCP student. My mom and dad enrolled me in this school.

I was so autistic back then, I would not change my school uniform. I used to cry and throw a fit if anyone tried to change me into the school's uniform. Now I think it's kind of silly but looking back I feel bad for myself.

I still remember vividly the first day at my new school. My parents and the headteacher came to an agreement on moving me down a year, due to my missing that year of learning because I learned very little at my old school. So, I was really two to three years behind and with my autism my brain tended to process things slower than other people. So, catching up would be really hard. Consequently, I started in reception.

I remember my first day so well. It was definitely better for my learning. When Covid hit, I missed another two years of learning but so did the other kids. It was stressful being back at school after Covid. My parents insisted I moved back up into the year I was supposed to be in.

I knew no one in that class so it was awkward at first. I was always the kid with the lowest test score back then I got around ten percent on most things. For maths, they did Whiterose Maths, told us to read the question, expected us to know it and have a competition with the whole class to see who would answer it first. Some kids learn like that but kids like me certainly don't .

Despite all my struggles, I passed an entrance exam for a private secondary school and I'm in the year group I'm supposed to be in. My mum and dad are so proud of me.

Overall, my life is all good. I am a Tae Kwon-do world champion, which is my biggest achievement so far. Exercise is my release.

I'm slowly catching up with my studies, and instead of ten percent, I'm now getting between fifteen percent and fifty percent.

The only thing that's hard is that sometimes people don't understand me. For example, if I ask them to repeat because I might miss-hear what they have said. They quite often might say "What's wrong? Are you deaf?" and they won't repeat again as they get fed up. This has led to my upset being left out of things, struggling to take part with others, which mentally/emotionally affects my confidence in many ways.

I love football, karate, Tae Kwon-do, drama and seeing friends at the weekends.

People often ask me how it feels to not hear. I could never really answer that until I got my 'waterproof' ears. When I went under the water it sounded the same blurry silence. So now when people ask, I say to them, "You know when you go in the water? Underneath that is what it sounds like."

That's another reason why I love the beach, sea and pool so much because they understand me. ☺

Many thanks for reading. Hope this helps

Waterproof implants

Frank English
Author

Born in 1946 in the West Riding of Yorkshire's coal fields around Wakefield, he attended grammar school, where he enjoyed sport rather more than academic work. After three years at teacher training college in Leeds, he became a teacher in 1967. He spent a lot of time during his teaching career entertaining children of all ages, a large part of which was through telling stories, and encouraging them to escape into a world of imagination and wonder. Some of his most disturbed youngsters he found to be very talented poets, for example. He has always had a wicked sense of humour, which has blossomed only during the time he has spent with his wife, Denise. This sense of humour also allowed many youngsters to survive often difficult and brutalising home environments.

In 2006, he retired after forty years working in schools with young people who had significantly disrupted lives because of behaviour disorders and poor social adjustment, generally brought about through circumstances beyond their control. At the same time as moving from leafy lane suburban middle-class school teaching in Leeds to residential schooling for emotional and behavioural disturbance in the early 1990s, changed family circumstance provided the spur to achieve ambitions. Supported by his wife, Denise, he achieved a Master's degree in his mid-forties and a PhD at the age of fifty-six, because he had always wanted to do so.

Now enjoying glorious retirement, he spends as much time as life will allow writing, reading and travelling.

Other books for adults he has written:
Jack the Lad	Published 2016
Jack	Published 2016
Hit the Road Jack	Published 2017

Welcome Back Jack	Published 2017
All Right Jack?	Published 2019
Carry On Jack	Published 2020
Where to Now, Jack?	Published 2022
Hidden Secrets	Published 2021
Secrets Revealed	Published 2022
No More Secrets	Published 2023
And Now…	Published 2025

Children's books he has written to date:

Magic Parcel: The Awakening	Published June 2010
Magic Parcel: The Gathering Storm	Published March 2011
Magic Parcel: A New Dawn	Published August 2012
18 Mulberry Road	Published September 2011
25 Primrose Walk	Published January 2013
Autumn Adventures	Published September 2013
Winter Tales	Published September 2014
Towards Spring	Published September 2016
Juniper's Tale	Published August 2018
Honey	Published January 2019
The Story of Lemuel Pecker	Published April 2019
Josephine's Journey	Published June 2019
Holly's Prize	Published April 2020
Garnett's Grand Getaway	Published May 2020
Sara's Astonishing Story	Published June 2020

The Boys in Black — Published August 2020
The Magic Whistle and the Tiny Bag of Wishes — Published October 2020
Half Moon Farm — Published March 2021
The Spirit Tree — Published February 2022
Mabel's Miraculous Manner — Published September 2022
Amalie's Amazing Adventures — Published September 2023
Believe — Published October 2023
The Adventures of the Lofthouse Family — Published June 2024